HAL LEONARD

BARITONE UKULELE BOOK 1

UKULELE METHOD

BY LIL' REV

ISBN 978-1-4584-0487-9

In Australia Contact:
Hal Leonard Australia Pty. Ltd.
4 Lentara Court
Cheltenham, Victoria, 3192 Australia
Email: ausadmin@halleonard.com.au

Visit Hal Leonard Online at **www.halleonard.com**

HAL•LEONARD®
CORPORATION
7777 W. BLUEMOUND RD. P.O. BOX 13819 MILWAUKEE, WI 53213

INTRODUCTION

Welcome to the *Hal Leonard Baritone Ukulele Method Book 1.* This method has been designed to help you achieve a beginner's level of mastery on the baritone ukulele. We'll explore note reading, tablature, basic melody playing, strumming, standard right-hand strokes, essential strums, and ukulele history.

Once you begin, you will find that, like all members of the ukulele family, the baritone has a certain magic about it that almost always seems to attract a smile from those on the receiving end of its joyful noise.

Because the baritone is tuned like the top four strings on the guitar (D–G–B–E), it's a great stepping stone on one's path towards guitar studies. I cannot stress this enough though: the baritone is more than capable of standing on its own two feet—be it jazz, chord-melody, fingerpicking, blues, rock, pop, country, or any other genre that one might enjoy playing. Indeed, one could make a lifelong pursuit of baritone mastery and still have plenty to learn. The sky is the limit!

I've designed this manual to gradually progress as you move through the book, so it's advised that you start at the beginning and work through it in order. This book uses a variety of musical examples to help you grow as a baritone player. There are plenty of basic folk songs for beginners, and eventually we move on to holiday, rock, blues, rockabilly, historical, minstrel, old-timey, bluegrass, and early country.

Good luck and happy strumming (and picking)!

ABOUT THE AUTHOR

Lil' Rev is the author of *The Hal Leonard Ukulele Method Books 1 & 2* as well as *101 Ukulele Licks, Easy Songs for Ukulele*, and *Play Harmonica Today* (all published by Hal Leonard). He stays busy touring North America as a traveling clinician and performer. You can learn more about Lil' Rev, his books, awards, and tour schedule by visiting *www.lilrev.com* or *http://fountainofuke.blogspot.com/*.

The author wishes to thank the following people for their help with this book: Will Branch (editing), Michael Nepper (photos), and Jenn Rupp (Finale, typesetting, and editing).

ABOUT THE AUDIO

The audio accompanying this book contains recordings of select exercises and tunes within the lessons. Wherever you see an audio icon (🔊), play the corresponding track number. Your goal should be to learn the piece well enough to play along with the recorded uke. Many examples have both chords and melodies written out, so you can play one part while the recorded uke plays the other.

Recorded at Velvet Sky, Milwaukee, WI

Engineered by Scott Finch

Performed by Lil' Rev

A BRIEF HISTORY OF THE BARITONE UKULELE

Unlike the soprano, concert, and tenor-sized ukulele, the baritone is a relative latecomer in the history of the instrument. The late 1870s is the most often-cited time of our beloved ukulele's humble beginning, though the baritone didn't enter the fray until circa 1949–1950. Most instrument stories tend to take on a life of their own as they are filtered through the generations. Folklore is rife with embellishment, and one would think that this might apply to the baritone as well. But so far as I can see, all paths lead back to the Favilla Brothers Instrument Company of Brooklyn, New York.

The Favilla Brothers, John and Joseph, started building soprano ukuleles in the late 1890s, eventually adding concert, tenor, and finally the baritone in 1949. As the Favilla Company was also adept at building guitars, the baritone became the company's obvious answer for those to whom the guitar was too cumbersome, including kids and women who didn't quite feel comfortable with a standard dreadnaught or archtop-sized guitar in their hands.

Jason Mraz

Photo by Bill Zelman

While other brands like Vega and Regal almost immediately followed suit, by the 1960s even the prestigious uke manufacturer Martin Guitar Company had begun building baritones in response to the burgeoning folk revival—a time that would much later find Joni Mitchell, Carole King, Pat Boone, Scatman Crothers, and George Harrison with ukuleles in their hands.

Arthur Godfrey

Photo courtesy of Library of Congress/New York–World Telegram and the Sun Newspaper Photograph Collection

By far the most visible baritone ukulele player to date has been Arthur Godfrey. In fact, a good deal of literature implies that he invented the instrument—a claim that is completely refutable! Nevertheless, as the biggest TV and radio uke star of the 1950s, Arthur Godfrey undeniably helped spread the joy of the baritone far and wide.

Today, the baritone can be seen and heard all over the blogosphere, with sites like Humble Baritonics and YouTube featuring tons of history and performance. I think it's safe to say that the baritone uke has finally come into its own!

YOUR BARITONE UKULELE

The baritone ukulele comes in many different styles and shapes. What they all have in common is a 14-fret neck (to the body) and a D–G–B–E (low to high) tuning. Today, you can find everything from baritone banjo ukes, resonator baritones, solid-body electric baritones, cutaway baritones, and even flying V baritones! Most baritones range in price from $150 (on the cheap side) all the way up to $2,000. Some companies a beginning uke student can count on are Ohana, Kala, Kamaka, Ko'aloha, Lanikai, Mya-Moe, Tony Graziano, and Da Silva Ukuleles, to name a few. (Some of these companies carry high-end ukes as well.)

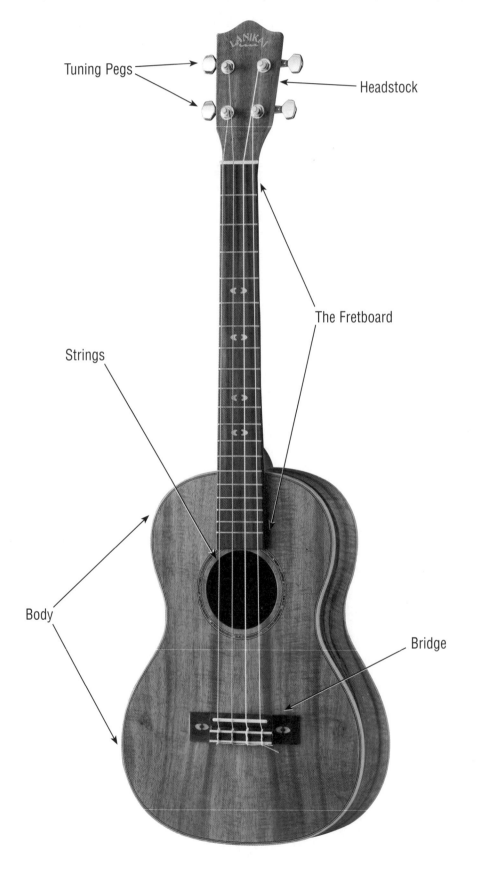

Tuning Pegs

Headstock

The Fretboard

Strings

Body

Bridge

TUNING

When you tune your ukulele, you will adjust the **pitch** (highness or lowness) of each individual string using the tuning pegs. When you tighten a string, you raise the pitch. When you loosen a string, you lower the pitch.

TUNING TO THE AUDIO

The strings on the baritone uke are numbered 1–4, with string 4 being closest to your chest. The baritone is tuned like the top four strings on the guitar (low to high in pitch):

TRACK 1

Pitch:	D	G	B	E
String:	4	3	2	1

Listen to the correct pitches given on the audio (Track #1) and gently turn the tuning pegs until the sound of each string matches that of the audio.

TUNING WITH AN ELECTRONIC TUNER

An electronic tuner will "hear" whether or not your strings are in tune, allowing you to correct the pitch. While I advocate learning how to tune by ear (being able to recognize and match the sound of a pitch without the help of a machine), an electronic tuner can be really handy when you are just starting out and have not yet developed the ability to recognize an in-tune pitch.

An electronic tuner is also helpful when you are in a room with a lot of ambient noise.

RELATIVE TUNING

Ideally, if you do not have an electronic tuner, you would have a piano, tuning fork, or pitch pipe from which to get a good reference note. However, sometimes these may not be available. Often you may have to tune your instrument to itself when there is no other source available. To do this, follow these steps:

1. Assume the fourth string is in tune (too low and it will buzz—too high and the string may break).

2. Put one finger down at the fifth fret of the D string and pluck the string; this will give you a G note. Continue to strike it and the open third string together. Adjust the open third string using the tuning peg until it matches the fourth-string note.

3. Once the third string is in tune, put one finger down at its fourth fret; this will give you a B note. Now pluck this string and match your open second string to this pitch.

4. Once the second string is in tune, put one finger down at its fifth fret; this will give you an E note. Pluck it and match the open first string to this pitch.

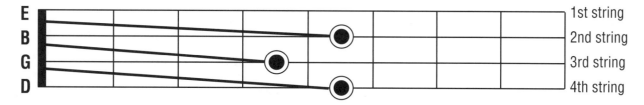

Great! Your baritone is now in tune!

PLAYING POSITION

There are a variety of different ways to hold the baritone ukulele comfortably. Typically, you will be seated, but some players prefer to stand up. If you decide that you would be more comfortable standing, you'll need to purchase a strap, but make sure that your ukulele has some strap buttons on it as well. Most stores carry these items and can help you to get started.

The seated baritone position is the easiest. Simply rest the uke on your right leg and apply a small amount of pressure with the right forearm to the baritone's upper bout, securing it gently against your rib cage.

The standing position takes a little more getting used to. As long as you use a strap, in time this will begin to feel very relaxed as well.

THE RIGHT HAND

Once you become comfortable holding your baritone uke, you'll need to become familiar with the proper hand, thumb, and finger positions for strumming and picking.

Hand

Most ukulele strumming happens over the fretboard at around the twelfth fret.

Thumb

The thumb is employed in many useful ways, including simple brush strokes. When you reach a more advanced level, it can be used for fingerpicking as well.

Finger

The squirt-gun shape is used to strum. Curl your right pointer finger inward and place it just over the twelfth fret.

MUSICAL SYMBOLS

Music is written with notes on a **staff**. The staff has five lines and four spaces between the lines. Where a note is written on the staff determines its pitch (highnes or lowness). At the beginning of the staff is a **clef sign**. Ukulele music written in the treble clef.

STAFF   **TREBLE CLEF**

Each line and space of the staff has a letter name. The **lines** are (from bottom to top) E–G–B–D–F, which you can remember as "**E**very **G**ood **B**oy **D**oes **F**ine." The **spaces** are (from bottom to top) F–A–C–E, which spells "face."

LINES   E   G   B   D   F   **SPACES**   F   A   C   E

The staff is divided into several parts by bar lines. The space between two bar lines is a called a **measure** (also known as a "bar"). At the end of a piece of music a double bar is placed on the staff.

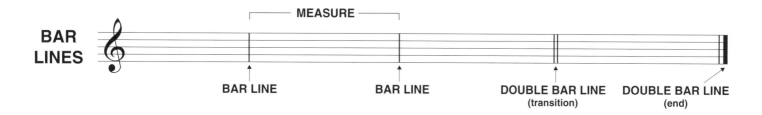

BAR LINES

MEASURE

BAR LINE   BAR LINE   DOUBLE BAR LINE   DOUBLE BAR LINE
                                         (transition)   (end)

Each measure contains a group of **beats**. Beats are the steady pulse of music. You respond to the pulse or beat when you tap your foot.

The two numbers placed next to the clef sign are the **time signature**.
The top numbers tells you how many beats are in one measure.

FOUR BEATS PER MEASURE
QUARTER NOTE (♩) GETS ONE BEAT

The bottom number of the time signature tells you what kind of note will receive one beat.

Notes indicate the length (number of counts) of a musical sound.

NOTE VALUES   𝅝   𝅗𝅥   ♩

WHOLE NOTE = 4 BEATS   HALF NOTE = 2 BEATS   QUARTER NOTE = 1 BEAT

When different kinds of notes are placed on different lines or spaces, you will know the pitch of the note and how long to play the sound.

TIES, RESTS & TIME SIGNATURES

Before we start to get into some really great music, let's take a moment to familiarize ourselves with a few standard music symbols that you'll encounter as you work your way through this book.

RESTS

Music is made up of both sound and silence. Silence is represented by musical symbols called **rests**. They are just as important as the notes you play. Each type of note has a corresponding rest of the same name and duration:

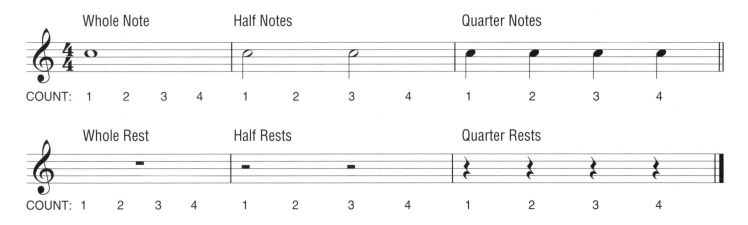

DOTTED NOTES

When you see a **dotted note**, hold that note 50% longer than you would normally hold it. For example, a dotted half note (♩.) lasts as long as a half note plus a quarter note. A dot adds half the value of the note.

TIES

Another standard music symbol that you will often encounter is the **tie** (⌒). When you see two notes tied together (♩⌒♩), play them as a single note. In other words, you simply add the first note to the second and hold them out for the full duration of both notes. (Ties can even extend through multiple measures.)

TIME SIGNATURES

A **time signature** tells you how the music in a song is counted. In a time signature, the top note tells you how many beats there are in a measure, and the bottom note tells which type of note gets one beat. This book will focus on two different time signatures: 4/4 and 3/4.

4/4 is the most common type of time signature. It tells us that there are four beats in a measure, and the quarter note is counted as one beat. We count: 1–2–3–4, 1–2–3–4, etc.

3/4 is the second most common time signature used in this book. It tells us that there are three beats in a measure, and the quarter note is counted as one beat. We count: 1–2–3, 1–2–3, etc. 3/4 is often referred to as "waltz time" because of its association with that style. It has that "oom–pah–pah" feel to it.

NOTES ON THE E STRING

We'll begin by learning notes on the E or first string. To fret a note, depress the string just behind the metal fret wire and not directly on it. Practice these notes slowly and repeat the name of each note as you play them. This will really help facilitate your memorization of the basic starting notes.

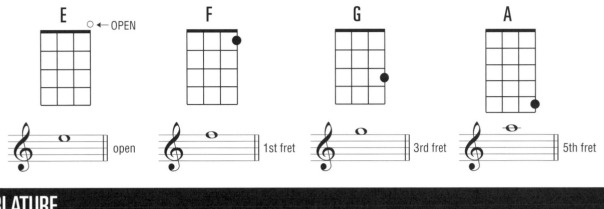

TABLATURE

In **tablature** (or tab) notation, the horizontal lines represent strings, and the numbers indicate which fret to play (0 = open). You'll always see the tab under the main staff.

Play these whole notes with your thumb and count "1–2–3–4," striking each note on the first beat of each measure and then counting "2–3–4."

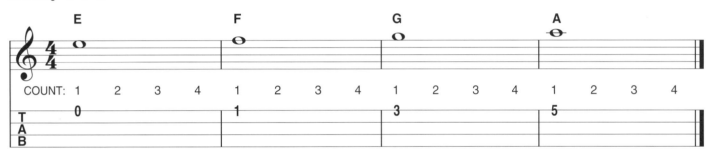

Now, try playing E, F, G, and A as half notes and count "1–2–3–4," striking each note on the first and third beat of each four-beat count per measure.

TRACK 2

Keep using your thumb and count "1–2–3–4" while playing these quarter notes. Remember: play one note for each of the four beats in a measure.

TRACK 3

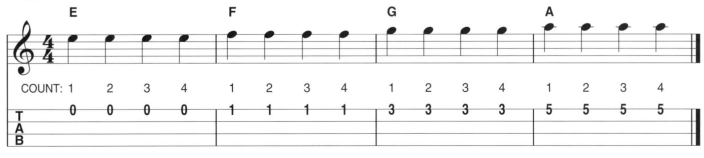

NOTES ON THE B STRING

Let's begin learning some of the notes on the B or second string.

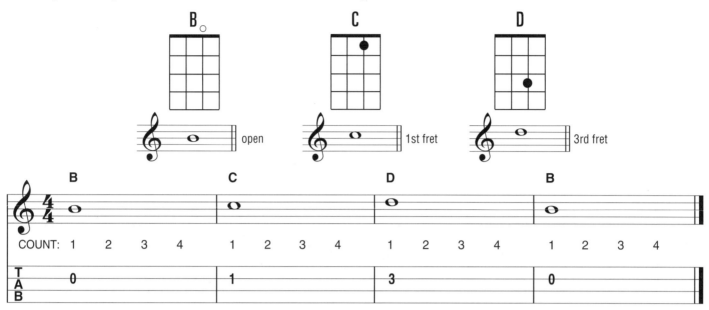

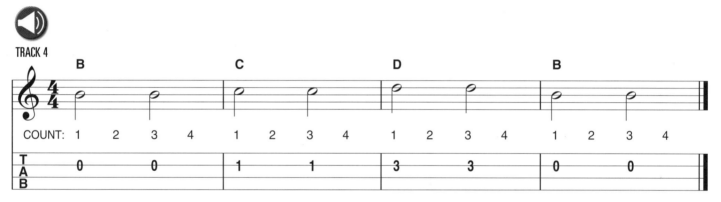

Now, try playing B, C, and D as half notes and count "1–2–3–4," striking each note on the first and third beat of each measure.

TRACK 4

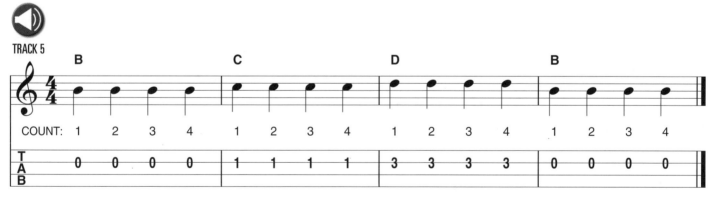

Keep using your thumb and count "1–2–3–4" while playing these quarter notes. Remember: one note for each of the four beats in a measure.

TRACK 5

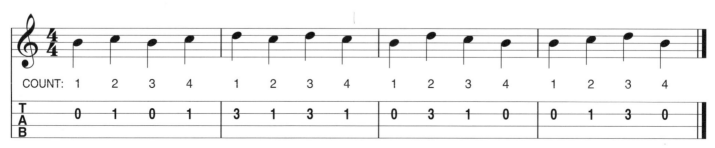

Good job! Let's mix up the order of the notes now.

This one includes notes on both the E and B strings.

B AND E STRING REVIEW

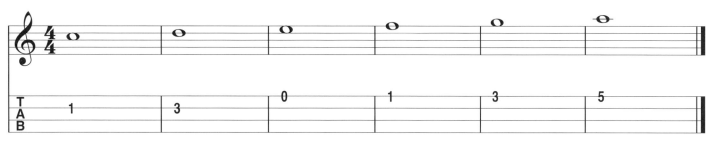

Here are two enduring classic melodies for you to practice playing the new notes. Gray **chord symbols** are used throughout this book to indicate the chords that back up your melody. They can be played by an instructor or another uke (or guitar) player.

 ## SKIP TO MY LOU

TRACK 6

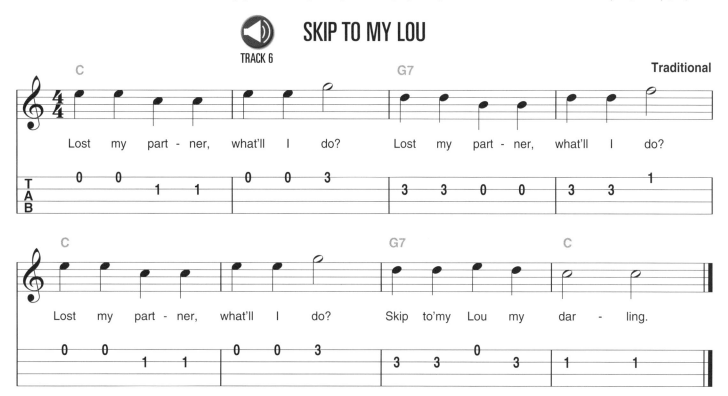

 ## MARY HAD A LITTLE LAMB

TRACK 7

Here's the good news! Age doesn't play a role in learning the baritone. Whether you are young or old, it's a great idea to start off with some of these classic American folk songs often heard in our grade school years. Once you've got some of these simple tunes under your fingers, you can then move on to rock, blues, boogie, pop, or anything else that you enjoy playing.

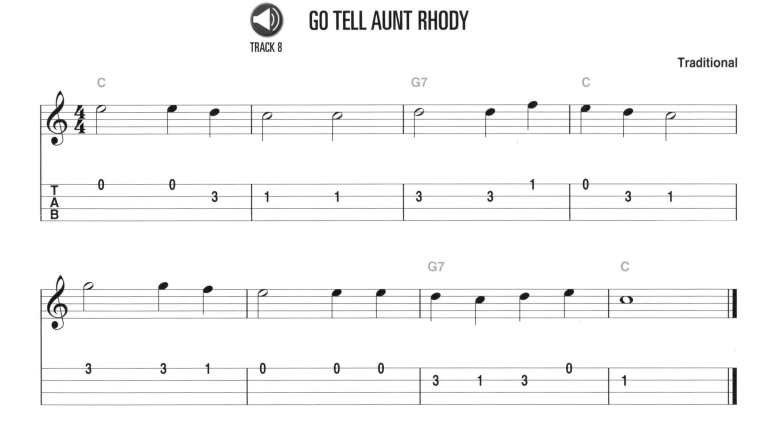

GO TELL AUNT RHODY

TRACK 8

Traditional

"Ode to Joy" is one of the classic instrumental arrangements taught to students of every instrument. It's great practice for playing quarter notes.

ODE TO JOY

TRACK 9

Ludwig van Beethoven

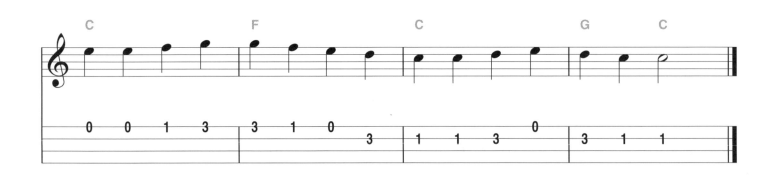

Everyone should know a few Christmas tunes.

JINGLE BELLS

TRACK 10

J. Pierpont

RIFFIN' ON LOUIE #1

TRACK 11

This exercise will continue our study of notes on the B and E strings. Look out for the quarter rest!

THE B & E ROCK

TRACK 12

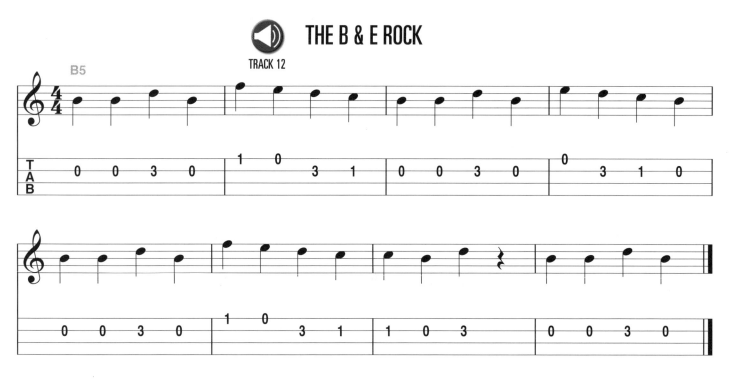

Now we'll add some dotted half notes and play in 3/4 time. So, count "1–2–3, 1–2–3."

Remember: When you see a dotted note, hold that note 50% longer than you would normally hold it. So, a dotted half note lasts as long as a half note plus a quarter note. Thus, a dot adds half the value of the note.

BEAUTIFUL BROWN EYES

TRACK 13

Traditional

NOTES ON THE G STRING

Now we will begin our study of the G string. You'll need to know three notes in order to work your way through the book: G, A, and B♭ (pronounced "B flat").

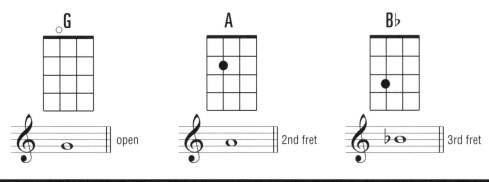

FLATS AND SHARPS

The symbol (♭) stands for **flat** and lowers the pitch by a half step (or one fret). When you see the flat symbol before a note on the staff, you lower that note by playing it down one fret. Conversely, when you see the **sharp** symbol (♯), you play that note one fret up.

Play these whole notes to begin.

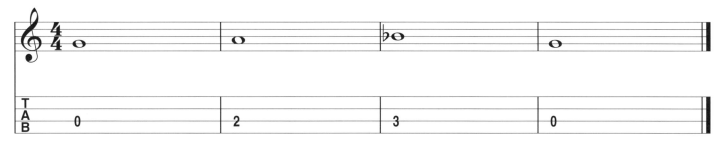

Now, let's integrate quarter notes and half notes.

TRACK 14

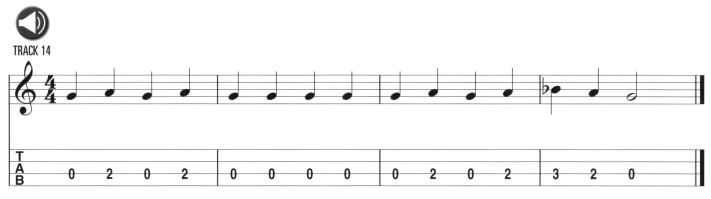

Once you are familiar with these notes, this exercise should flow along nicely.

TRACK 15

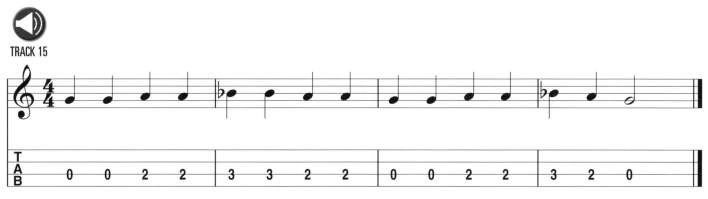

To finish, let's play an ascending G scale pattern. There's a new note on the first string in this example: F#. Because it is sharped, this note is one fret higher (played on the second fret) than the F note that you already know.

TRACK 16

This beautiful French melody dates back to the mid-18th century. It makes good practice when familiarizing yourself with the G and B strings.

AU CLAIR DE LA LUNE
(By the Light of the Moon)

French Folksong

This is a fun tune that will get you playing across all three strings.

SHORTENIN' BREAD

African-American Folksong

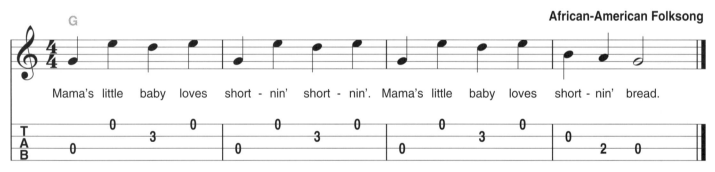

Mama's little baby loves short - nin' short - nin'. Mama's little baby loves short - nin' bread.

"Old Joe Clark" is a great workout in solidifying your knowledge of all three strings: E, B, and G. It's also good practice in playing quarter notes and half notes in a flowing manner.

OLD JOE CLARK

TRACK 17

Tennessee Folksong

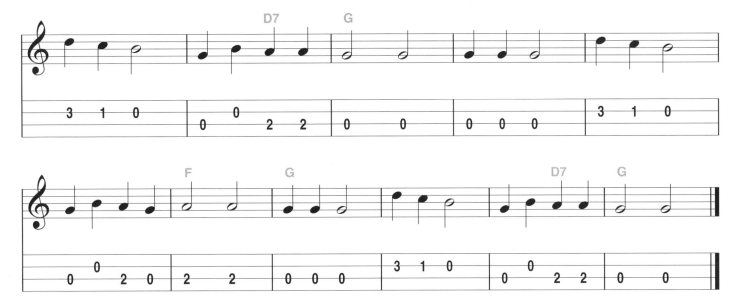

"Aura Lee" is both a beautiful folk melody and a pop tune made famous by Elvis Presley and recorded in 1956 as "Love Me Tender." For now, let's just concentrate on playing the melody; your teacher or fellow accompanist can play the chords for you. Later in the book, we'll begin to explore the C chord family more in depth.

AURA LEE

TRACK 18

George R. Poulton
and W.W. Fosdick

PICKUP NOTES

Often a piece of music won't begin on the first beat of the first measure. When this happens, these notes before the first full measure are called **pickup notes**; they appear in a partial measure called the **pickup measure**. Always remember to count the missing beats before playing your first pickup note. In some songs that begin with pickup notes, the last measure will be short the exact number of beats used as pickups. (This isn't always the case though.)

The pickup measure in this exercise has only one quarter note. Count "1–2–3" silently before playing the quarter note on beat 4. Notice that the last measure is short by one beat to balance out the one-beat pickup measure.

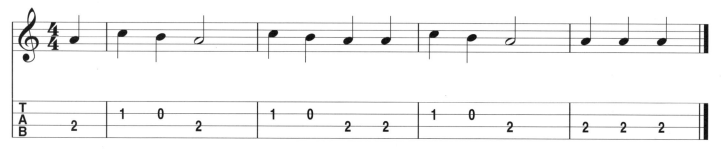

The following pickup measure has two quarter notes. Count "1–2" silently before playing beats 3 and 4.

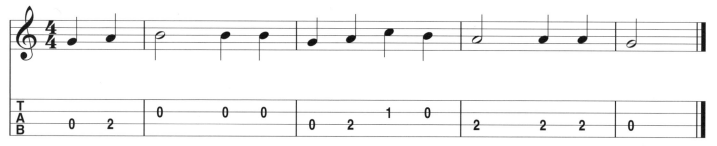

This last exercise begins on beat 4. Count "1–2–3" silently.

BUYING A BARITONE

Baritone ukuleles come in all shapes and sizes. Today, independent ukulele builders are creating some of the finest baritones ever made. As you become a better player, you may want to start looking for that perfect instrument. Here are five things to look for in a good baritone:

1) **Intonation**: Notes and chords, when fretted up and down the neck, sound consistently in tune and ring out clear and crisp without any obvious buzzing.

2) **Tuning**: The instrument has good tuners and is able to hold its pitch (stay in tune).

3) **Action**: The strings are not too high off the neck (making it hard to fret or chord).

4) **Look and Feel**: The instrument looks nice with a professional finish and plays well in your hands.

5) **Cost**: The price of a good baritone should range between $300 and $600. Sometimes you can find a nice old Regal, Favilla, or Martin on eBay or at a local flea market for almost nothing if you get lucky! Some of the higher-end builders that I recommend include Tony Graziano, Kerry Char, Mike Da Silva, or Mya-Moe.

Remember: with four beats per measure and three quarter notes to start, you come in on the second beat after counting the first beat silently. Watch out for the ties and dotted notes in this one!

WHEN THE SAINTS GO MARCHING IN

TRACK 19

Traditional

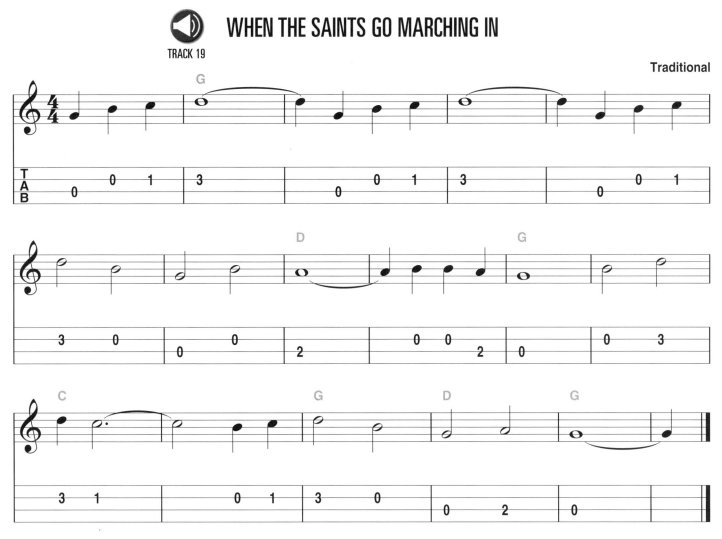

"O Happy Day" is the quintessential gospel song. It's a beautiful little melody that utilizes quarter notes, ties, and pickup notes. Count "1–2–3–4, 1" and then come in on the second beat to start the song. You can also just count "1" and then come in on beat 2, but counting a full measure first will give you a better sense of how the pickup notes work.

O HAPPY DAY

TRACK 20

Edward F. Rimbault and
Philip Doddridge

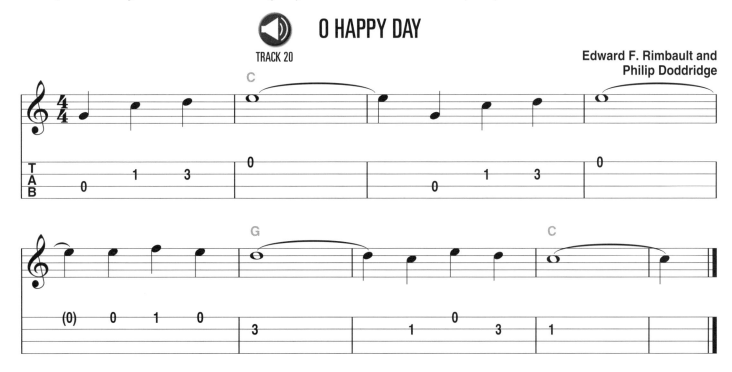

This beautiful cowboy melody will give you good practice in reading ties, pickup notes, and dotted notes. Listen to the audio a couple times to get the right feel.

THE RED RIVER VALLEY

TRACK 21

Traditional American Cowboy Song

Now that you are playing some melodies, let's get your fingers moving a bit more.

FINGERS-A-WALKING

TRACK 22

Watch the ties and remember to count.

SHE'LL BE COMIN' 'ROUND THE MOUNTAIN

TRACK 23

Traditional

Go cat go!

MAD TRAIN BOOGIE

TRACK 24

THE G CHORD FAMILY
G, G7, C, C7, D, D7, and Em Chords

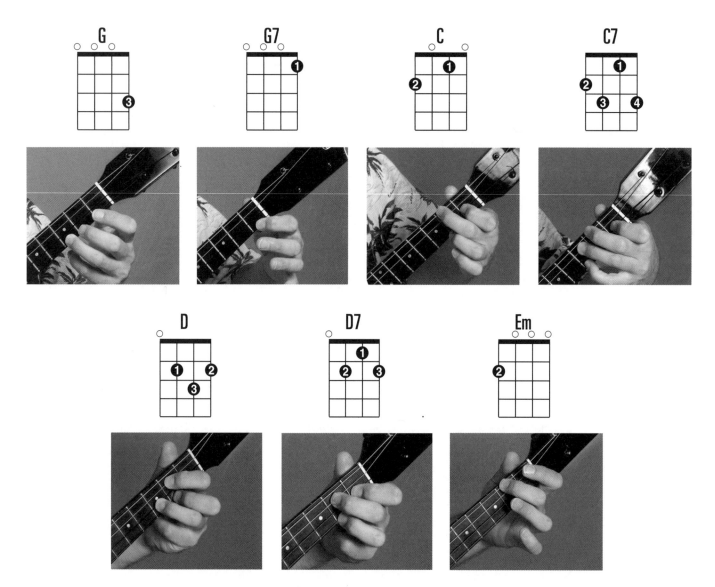

A **chord** is a combination of three or more notes played together. The chord grids above are like maps of your ukulele's fret-board. As you've seen with single notes, the dots show which strings to depress at which frets. The numbers on the dots tell you which fingers to use. To play the G chord, for example, use the tip of the third finger of your fretting hand and depress the E string just behind the third fret. Strum all four strings with your pointer finger, and voilà!

When we strum, we use our pointer finger to play **downstrokes** (strumming downward through the strings, toward the floor) and **upstrokes** (upward through the strings, toward the ceiling). Let's begin with a very basic two-chord exercise. Use a down, down, down-up, down strum pattern.

TRACK 25

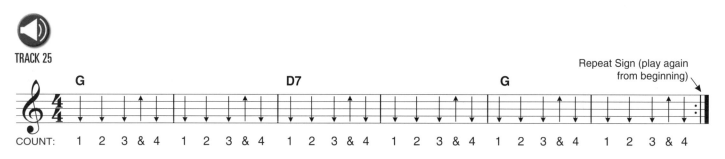

Repeat this progression until you can change chords smoothly.

TRACK 26

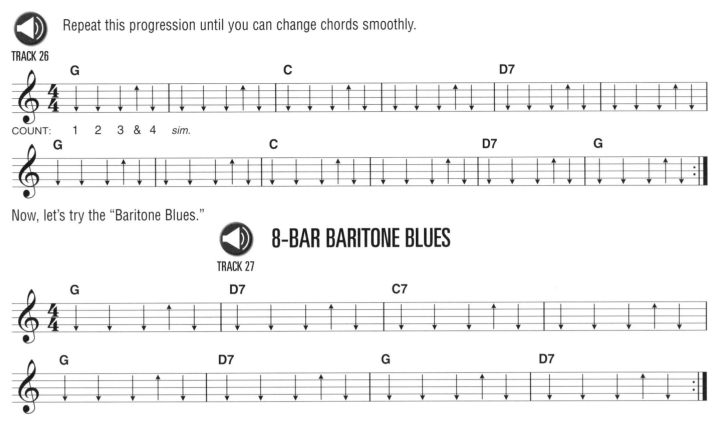

COUNT: 1 2 3 & 4 *sim.*

Now, let's try the "Baritone Blues."

8-BAR BARITONE BLUES

TRACK 27

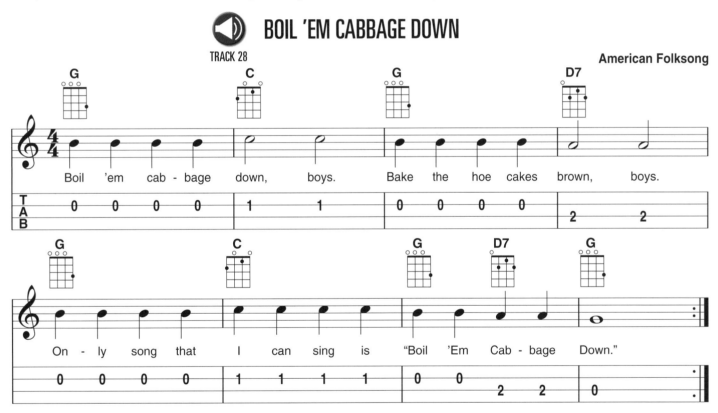

First, become comfortable with this melody. Then, go back and learn the rhythm part by strumming the chords.

BOIL 'EM CABBAGE DOWN

TRACK 28

American Folksong

Boil 'em cab - bage down, boys. Bake the hoe cakes brown, boys.

On - ly song that I can sing is "Boil 'Em Cab - bage Down."

COUNTRY UKE

The ukulele has a rich and storied history in American country music. While some perhaps don't think of the ukulele as an instrument capable of playing reels, squares, hoedowns, breakdowns, polkas, waltzes, and tough-luck ballads, recorded history can prove otherwise. Not only did the ukulele provide dance accompaniment for the hula in Hawaii, but on the mainland, it became a central part of the string and jug band era of the 1920s and 1930s. There have been many wonderful recordings over the years, by such acts as the Fiddling Powers Family, the Hillbillies, the Stoneman Family, Jimmie Rodgers, and many more. So, the next time you bring your ukulele to a bluegrass jam and start ripping through "Boil 'Em Cabbage Down," just know you are walking in the footsteps of ukulele giants from our countrified past.

JUST FUN STRUMMING IN G

Here's a set of some fun old-time tunes and bluegrass numbers that everyone loves to hear. Learn to play them by heart, and you'll be the life of the party, picnic, barbeque, or open mic! Here are the chords you'll be using. Notice that the A chord is one you haven't learned yet:

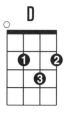 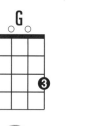 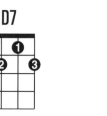 A

 HANDSOME MOLLY (4/4)

TRACK 29   **Bluegrass**

G   **D7**
Wish I was in London or some other seaport town.
                                G
Set my foot on a steamboat, I'd sail the ocean 'round.
                              D7
Sailing 'round the ocean, sailing 'round the sea,
                              G
Think of handsome Molly wherever she may be.
                                   D7
Don't you remember Molly, you gave me your right hand,
                              G
Said if ever you'd marry, that I'd be your man.
                              D7
Sailing 'round the ocean, sailing 'round the sea,
                              G
Think of handsome Molly wherever she may be.

 LITTLE BIRDIE (4/4)

TRACK 30   **Traditional**

G   **D7**   **G**
Little birdie, little birdie, come sing me your song.
                            D7   **G**
Got a short time to be here, and a long time to be gone.
                            D7   **G**
Rather be in some dark holler, where the sun don't never shine
                            D7   **G**
Than to see you with another, when you promised to be mine.

 MY BONNIE LIES OVER THE OCEAN (3/4)

TRACK 31   **Traditional**

G   **C**   **G**   **A**   **D**
My Bonnie lies over the ocean, my Bonnie lies over the sea.
       G   **C**   **G**   **C**   **D**   **G**
My Bonnie lies over the ocean; oh bring back my Bonnie to me.
             C   **D**   **G**
Bring back, oh bring back, bring back my Bonnie to me, to me.
             C   **D**   **G**
Bring back, oh bring back, oh bring back my Bonnie to me.

Use these exercises to improve your ability to change chords in the G chord family quickly and smoothly without breaking your rhythm. Both are presented with strumming arrows and tablature.

MR. HOLLY'S BARITONE ROCK

TRACK 32

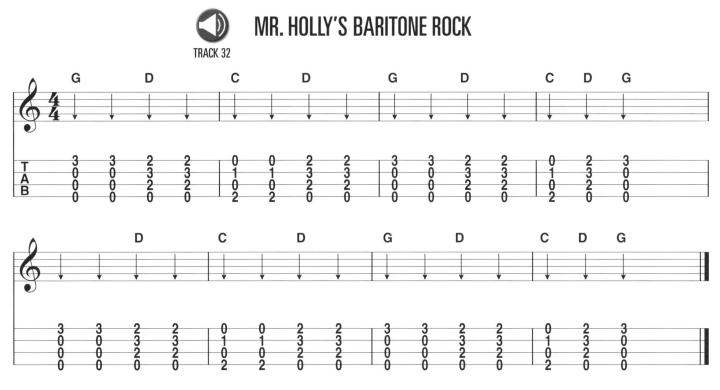

"8th of January" makes a nice little strumming exercise that will familiarize you with the classic down, down, down-up-down ukulele strum. In the process, it will also solidify your attempts to become more familiar with the G chord family.

8TH OF JANUARY

TRACK 33

Traditional

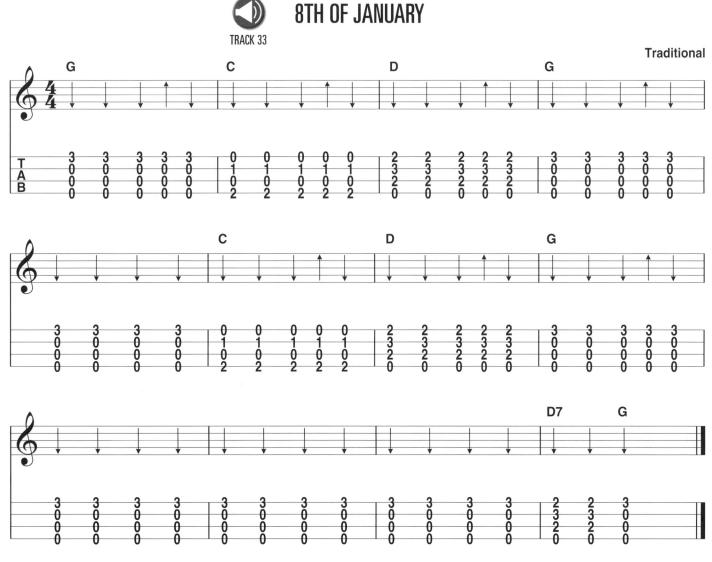

THE SINGLE ROLL STROKE

The **single roll stroke** is a lively rhythmic strumming technique that emphasizes the downbeat of the strum by unraveling your right-hand fingers one by one. When properly executed, it should sound like one continuous flowing beat.

Think of flicking a tiny ball of paper off of a desk. Now imagine lining up four tiny balls of paper and flicking each one with the pinky finger, ring finger, middle finger, and pointer finger, one after the next. Once you get good at this, it sounds like one continuous stroke and serves to punctuate your strums with a progressive rhythmic punch that really brings out the full sound of the ukulele.

In addition to roll strokes, there are many exciting right-hand techniques that you should pursue, including the two-finger roll, the five-finger roll, triple strokes, and even strums like George Formby's "fan stroke" or "split stroke." Lastly, these right-hand strokes lie at the heart of what is truly *the* ukulele sound! To really get a sense of what I am talking about, you should supplement this lesson with visuals and try to find some of the old footage of Roy Smeck, George Formby, or the slew of great Vaudeville-era performers on the Internet. Many instructors offer YouTube videos for the beginning ukulele student; I encourage you to seek these out and continue to develop your right-hand techniques.

Ok! Let's begin:

1) Bring your right-hand pinky down across all four strings.

2) Let your third finger follow right after your pinky.

3) Now your second (middle) finger follows
down across all four strings.

4) Finally, bring your pointer finger down
across all of the strings.

UKULELE FESTIVALS

Presently, in the U.S. alone there are at least a dozen annual ukulele festivals—from New York, Milwaukee, and Reno to Cerritos, Tampa, and Portland. There is nothing more inspiring than a weekend of jamming, studying, networking, and concertizing all things ukulele. It's well worth the cost of the trip, and you'll acquire a world of information with which to grow as a player! Seek and ye shall find!

EIGHTH NOTES

We're about to encounter some examples and tunes with **eighth notes**. You actually just played some eighth notes in the strum patterns you used in the last chapter. Now we'll take a closer look at them. Two eighth notes equal one quarter note in value.

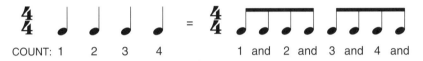

One eighth note is written with a **flag** (♪). Consecutive eighth notes are connected with a **beam** (♫). To count eighth notes, say "and" in between the beats. In 4/4 time, there are eight eighth notes in a measure, so we count "1 and 2 and 3 and 4 and," etc.

Try these eighth notes. Go slowly and evenly and count "1 and 2 and 3 and 4 and."

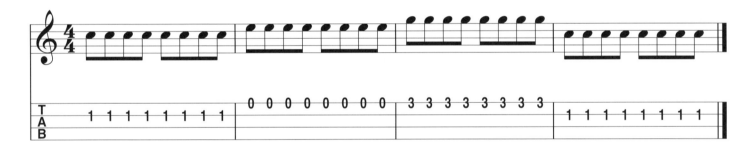

THE DRUNKEN SAILOR

TRACK 34

American Sea Chantey

"Stewball" is a folk song in 3/4 time, so remember there are three beats per measure. Count "ONE–two–three," or "OOM–pah–pah."

STEWBALL

Folk Song

Stew - ball was a good horse, and he held a high head. And the mane on his fore top was as fine as silk thread.

"Shortenin' Bread" is an old southern folk song and fiddle tune that you already played with quarter notes earlier in the book. Here, we start to get into some real eighth-note playing. Be sure to listen to the audio to get a good feel for this tune.

SHORTENIN' BREAD

TRACK 35

African-American Folksong

Ma-ma's lit - tle ba - by loves short - nin', short - nin'. Ma-ma's lit - tle ba - by loves short - nin' bread.

Ma-ma's lit - tle ba - by loves short - nin', short - nin'. Ma-ma's lit - tle ba - by loves short - nin' bread.

If you enjoy playing tunes with a real eighth-note feel, bluegrass, country, and old-time styles are full of this kind of musical symmetry. Fiddle tunes in particular will really instill a good sense of eighth-note playing as you develop. Learn a couple of these tunes, and you'll really be doing your right and left hands a favor. Examples would include "Turkey in the Straw," "Golden Slippers," "Arkansas Traveler," "Cripple Creek," and "Soldier's Joy," to name a few.

"Cluck Old Hen" is a classic old-time and bluegrass tune that offers a lot of bang for the buck. This song is a ton of fun to play once you get it down. It employs the use of rests and eighth notes. Have fun and keep those toes a-tappin'.

CLUCK OLD HEN

TRACK 36

This is a time-honored bluegrass lick that would work well after "Cluck Old Hen." Watch the rest.

SHAVE 'N HAIRCUT

TRACK 37

KEY SIGNATURES

One convenient way to avoid assigning a sharp (♯) to every F in a piece of music is to simply put a sharp sign at the beginning of each staff. Then every time you see an F note, you play an F♯ instead. This is called a **key signature** and it works for all kinds of sharps and flats. The next song uses this key signature, which also tells you that the tune is in the key of G.

"Buffalo Gals" is an old-time square dance melody that your great grandparents probably knew well. This melody has been the basis for many commercials and has also appeared in countless movies. This is a nice easy tune with which to continue your eighth-note studies. Remember that the key signature tells you to play every F note in the song as an F#.

BUFFALO GALS

TRACK 38

John Hodges

Some other tunes you might enjoy learning along the lines of "Buffalo Gals" include "Liza Jane," "Black-Eyed Susie," "Fly Around My Pretty Little Miss," "Ground Hog," "Sandy Boys," and "Them Golden Slippers."

PRACTICING

Regular practice is essential. Practicing a half hour each day is better than practicing two hours every four days. Find a regular time that works for you.

When you practice the exercises and songs, start very slowly at first and then gradually build up speed. You might enjoy playing with a **metronome**, which helps you keep time and also teaches you to play along with a steady beat. In addition to playing along with the audio, metronome practice will really help you develop a strong sense of rhythm prior to jamming with others. You can purchase an inexpensive metronome at almost any music store.

THE C CHORD FAMILY
C, C7, F, F7, G, G7, and Am

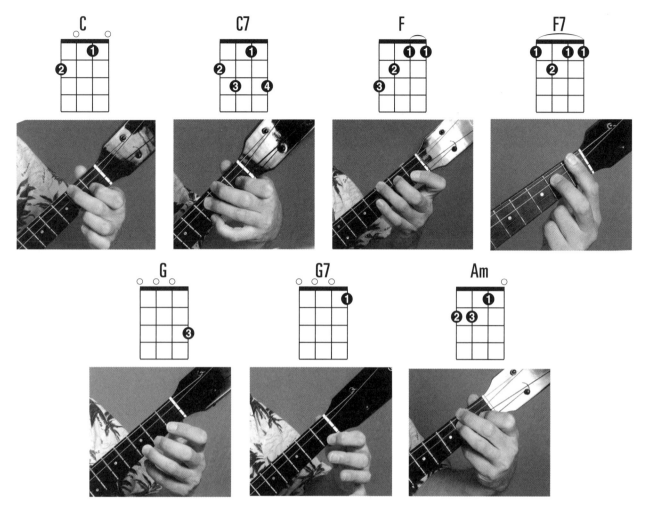

Notice that the F and F7 chords require you to **barre** multiple notes with one finger. This means you need to lay your index finger flat across several strings at a time. Study the photos to see how this is done.

TRACK 39

To begin, let's start out with a basic C and G7 chord progression. On all of these exercises we'll use the strum pattern: down, down, down, down.

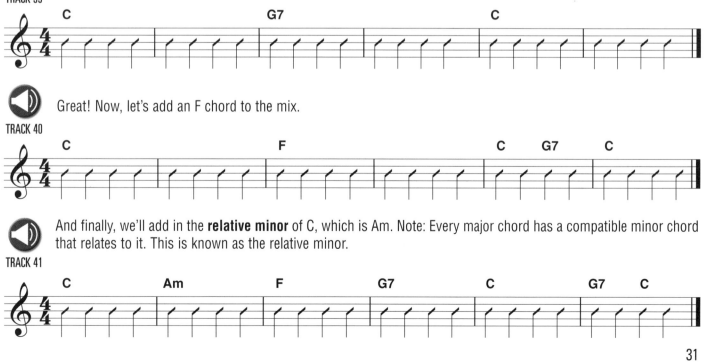

JUST FUN STRUMMING IN C

Here is another fun set. This time, we'll take on some time-honored kid's tunes. Here are the chords you'll be using:

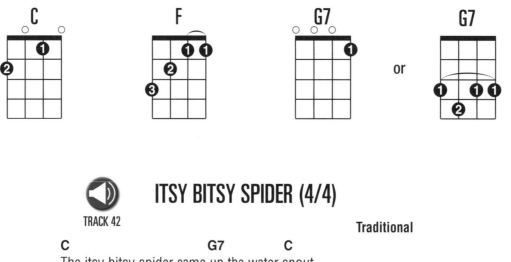

 ITSY BITSY SPIDER (4/4)

TRACK 42

Traditional

C   G7   C
The itsy bitsy spider came up the water spout.
          G7   C
Down came the rain and washed the spider out.
         G7   C
Out came the sun and dried up all the rain.
            G7   C
And the itsy bitsy spider climbed up the spout again.

 JIM ALONG JOSIE (4/4)

TRACK 43

American Folk Song

C   F C   G7   C
Jumping along, Jim along Josie, jumping along, Jim along Joe.
      F C   G7   C
Running along, Jim along Josie, running along, Jim along Joe.
       F   C   G7   C
Crawling around, Jim along Josie, crawling around, Jim along Joe.
      F   C   G7   C
Hopping around, Jim along Josie, hopping around, Jim along Joe.
      F   C   G7   C
Jumping along, Jim along Josie, jumping along, Jim along Joe.

C CHORD FAMILY STRUMMING EXERCISES

Here's a funky little exercise to help you get familiar with the C chord family.

THE BARITONE TWIST

TRACK 44

Here's another C chordal exercise.

NEW ORLEANS BARITONE BOP #1

TRACK 45

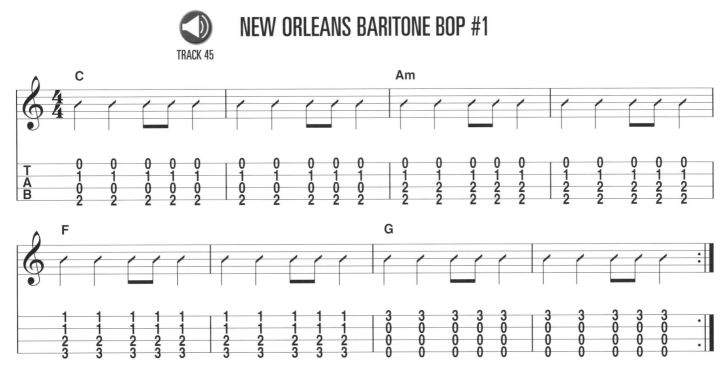

Learning how to smoothly transition between chords should be your top priority.

NEW ORLEANS BARITONE BOP #2

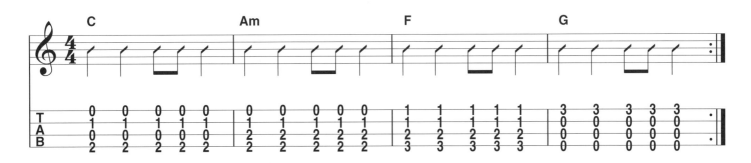

PLAYING TREMOLO

Tremolo is a standard right-hand technique employed by ukulele players the world over. It makes a really nice alternative to strumming, and it's well worth the effort to integrate this into your daily practice. Here's how it's done:

1) Spread the fingers of your right hand as shown.

2) Position your pointer over the tenth fret.

3) Using the pad of your fingertip, gently yet rapidly rub all four strings in a continuous and even up-and-down motion.

Now let's try a basic three-chord progression using tremolo.

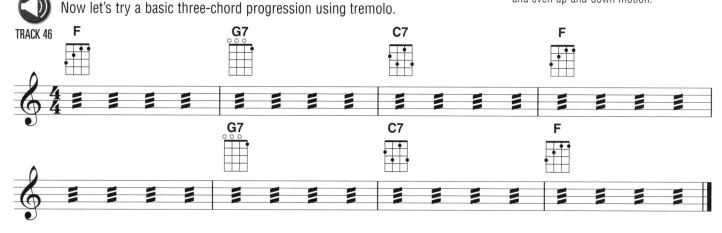

TRACK 46

Go back to page 17 and review the melody for "Aura Lee." Once you have it in your head, play this chord progression using tremolo. Earlier in the book, you focused on the individual notes; now you'll need to look closely at the chords, including the new E7 chord. Count "1–2–3–4" for each measure. Once you have it down, try playing this example along with audio Track #18.

AURA LEE

TRACK 47

George R. Poulton
and W.W. Fosdick

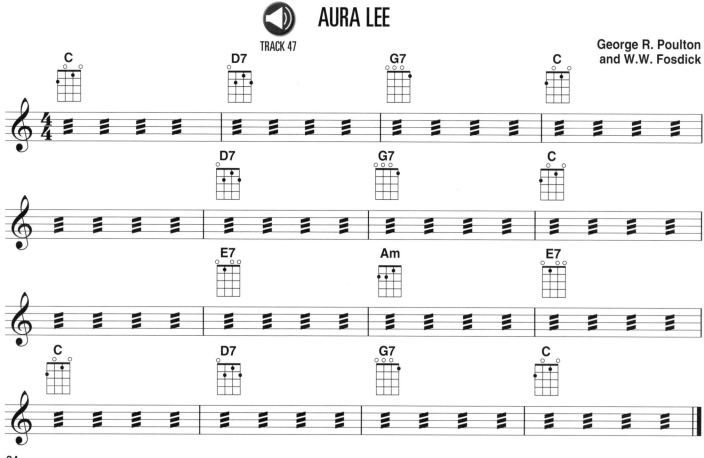

THE DOO-WOP CHORD CYCLE

The "doo-wop chord cycle" is a popular set of chord changes known to musicians the world over. It makes for great fun when working to perfect your right-hand tremolo technique. Likewise, it will help to build your chord vocabulary by leaps and bounds. There are literally hundreds of songs that use this sequence in one way or another. So, in practicing this exercise, not only are you developing your tremolo skill, but you'll also prepare yourself to sing and play hundreds of classics—from Sam Cooke's "You Send Me" and Bruce Channel's "Hey Baby" to the Five Satins' "In the Still of the Night" and the Shirelles' "Will You Love Me Tomorrow."

Every beginning baritone player yearns to jam with others and strum well enough to support a song. If this describes you, then you'll really want to take the time to learn this chord cycle in all five keys listed below. In doing so, your ability to play and change chords quickly will rapidly improve.

First, finger the new chords (Dm, Gm, Bm, A7, and F♯m) and gently strum them. Then, begin to try playing these progressions with tremolo, keeping a steady down-up motion going fluidly and constantly. If this is too hard for you, then just brush each chord with a downstroke—four beats to a measure.

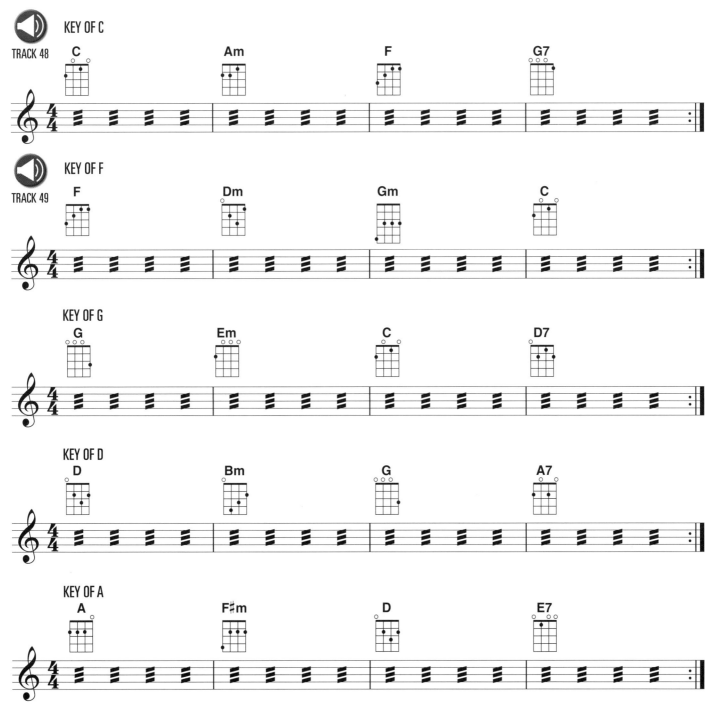

35

Start by resting the right thumb on the right pointer finger. With the thumb supporting that finger, gently move your finger in a down-up-down-up continuous motion. When you can do this smoothly with just the G chord, begin to try and follow the "Goodnight Ilene" chord progression. After a few practices, your tremolo will become more fluid, and soon you'll be able to play through the whole exercise without getting tired or breaking your rhythm.

GOODNIGHT ILENE

TRACK 50

THE D CHORD FAMILY
D, D7, G, G7, A, A7, and Bm

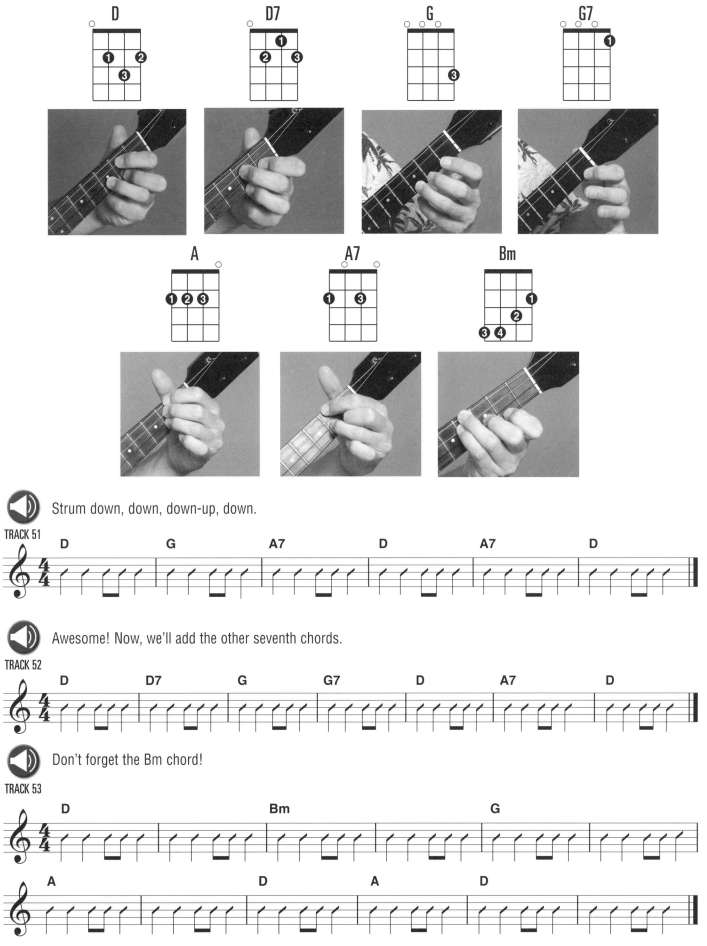

Strum down, down, down-up, down.

TRACK 51

| D | G | A7 | D | A7 | D |

Awesome! Now, we'll add the other seventh chords.

TRACK 52

| D | D7 | G | G7 | D | A7 | D |

Don't forget the Bm chord!

TRACK 53

| D | | Bm | | G | |

| A | | D | A | D | |

NOTES ON THE D STRING

Let's learn some of the notes on the D or fourth string. As always, we begin practicing these notes slowly at first and then gradually build up speed. Remember to say the name of each note as you fret it.

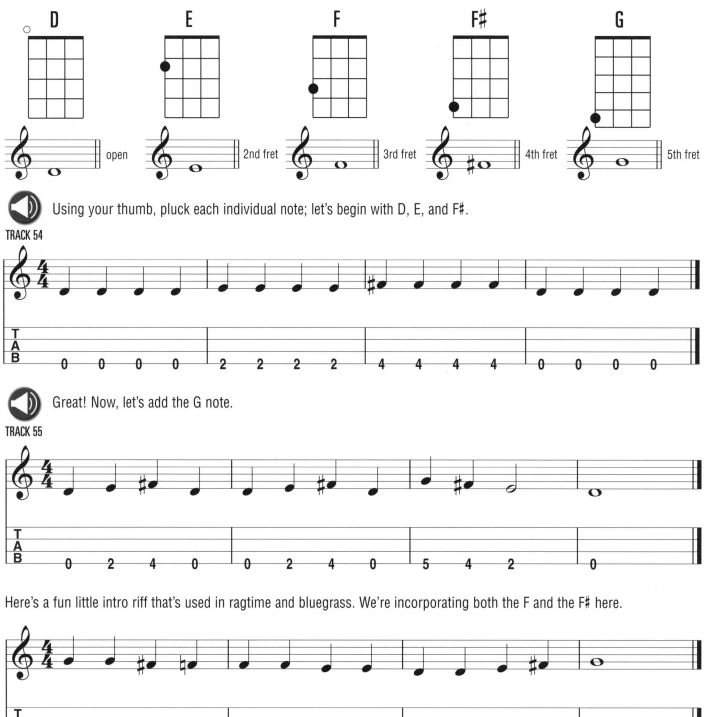

Using your thumb, pluck each individual note; let's begin with D, E, and F#.

TRACK 54

Great! Now, let's add the G note.

TRACK 55

Here's a fun little intro riff that's used in ragtime and bluegrass. We're incorporating both the F and the F# here.

Lastly, here's a little exercise to get you ready for the next couple of songs.

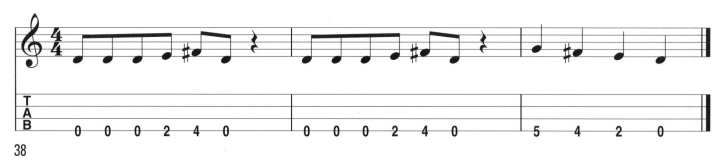

THE D MAJOR SCALE

Let's play the D major scale. Play this slowly one note at a time. Notice there are two sharps in the key signature. This means that every F and C in the scale should be sharped.

This tune will get you playing across all four strings in the D major scale. Remember the key signature! Play the chords as well.

WILDWOOD FLOWER

TRACK 56

Traditional

This song has a key signature for G major: only one sharp (F#).

TOM DOOLEY

Traditional

Hang down your head Tom Doo - ley. Hang down your head and cry.

Hang down your head Tom Doo - ley. Poor boy, you're bound to die.

This song only uses one note on the D string: the G note.

HEY LOLLY, LOLLY

TRACK 57

Calypso

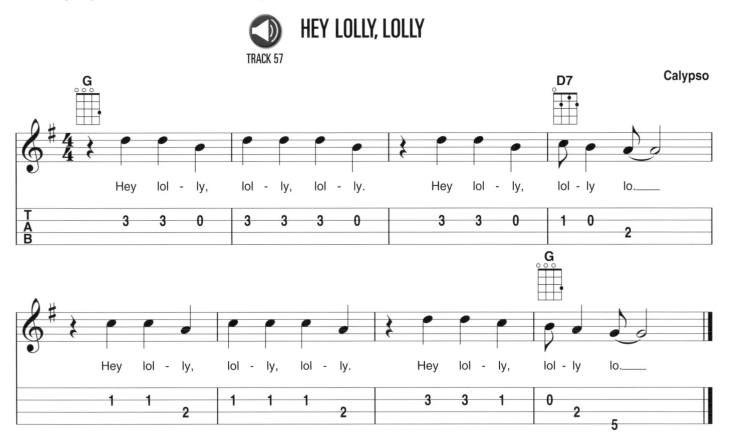

Hey lol - ly, lol - ly, lol - ly. Hey lol - ly, lol - ly lo.___

Hey lol - ly, lol - ly, lol - ly. Hey lol - ly, lol - ly lo.___

For the next example, put your hand on your heart and feel your heartbeat. It goes lub-DUB, lub-DUB. Now, let's practice our D-string notes and play the same pattern as our heartbeat. This will be a little trickier than the others due to the **syncopation** (stress of the weak beat). Count along to help feel the rhythm.

D HEARBEAT EXERCISE

TRACK 58

COUNT: 1 & (2) & 3 (4)   1 & (2) & 3 (4)   1 & (2) & 3 (4)   1 & (2) & 3 (4)   1 2 & 3 (4)

"Little Brown Jug" is a classic, old-timey, minstrel-era piece. This tune will help familiarize you with the F♯ and G notes on the D string.

LITTLE BROWN JUG

TRACK 59

Joseph E. Winner

Use this exercise to build speed and fretboard agility in **first position**. Playing in first position means that your first finger lines up with the first fret. We're covering a lot of notes here, so use the tab to help if necessary.

FINGER BUSTER #1
TRACK 60

These next two exercises are designed to familiarize you with the notes on the D string.

PETER'S GUN
TRACK 61

In this next song, the key signature is for the key of G. However, notice in the music that there are **natural signs** (♮) in front of the F notes. This tells us to ignore the key signature and play F instead of F♯. Why use the key signature then? Well, it lets the performer know that G is still the key of the song and should still feel like "home base."

ALMOST-A-BOOGIE
TRACK 62

The boogie woogie is one of the most exciting musical studies a beginning student can undertake. Not only does it stand alone, but it also lends itself well to jamming with others. In essence, it's a real classic piece of music. With a little practice and some listening to the audio, the beginning student can aspire to sounding like a real pro with "Big Bill's Baritone Boogie." Practice slowly at first, and then gradually build up speed. This piece will challenge you to play all four strings while also helping you to become adept at reading and playing eighth notes. Good luck and happy practicing!

TRACK 63

BIG BILL'S BARITONE BOOGIE

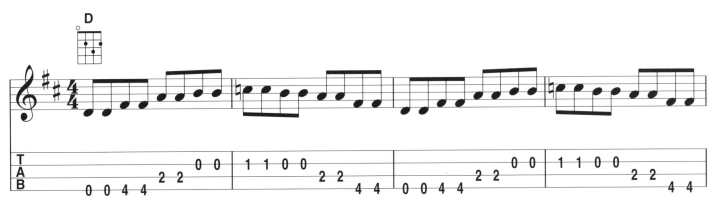

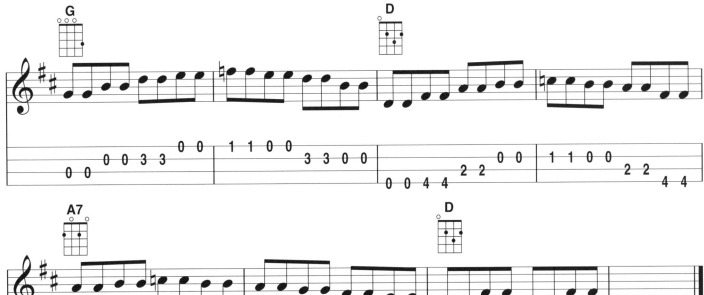

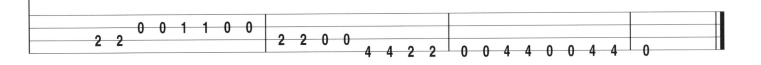

BOOGIE HISTORY

The boogie woogie is a style of music originally performed by African-American jazz, blues, and ragtime piano players. It provides a highly danceable groove that has, since its early development in the '20s, '30s, and '40s, become a definitive part of the American music vernacular. Today, you can hear elements of boogie woogie in country, rock, pop, blues, and even bluegrass. For further study, listen to the works of Memphis Slim, Roosevelt Sykes, Pinetop Perkins, Otis Spann, Little Brother Montgomery, Speckled Red, Professor Longhair, Doctor John, Leon Russell, and hundreds of other piano and bass players.

JUST FUN STRUMMING IN D

Here's another set of some great American chestnuts. These are all tunes that have really stood the test of time. First, give the audio a listen or two. Then try strumming along. Finally, if you are comfortable, sing and strum together. I've tried to keep the tune selection here basic so you could learn to become comfortable singing and strumming at the same time without being burdened by too many fancy chord changes. That will come in time! Here are the chords you'll be using. Notice the new E chord.

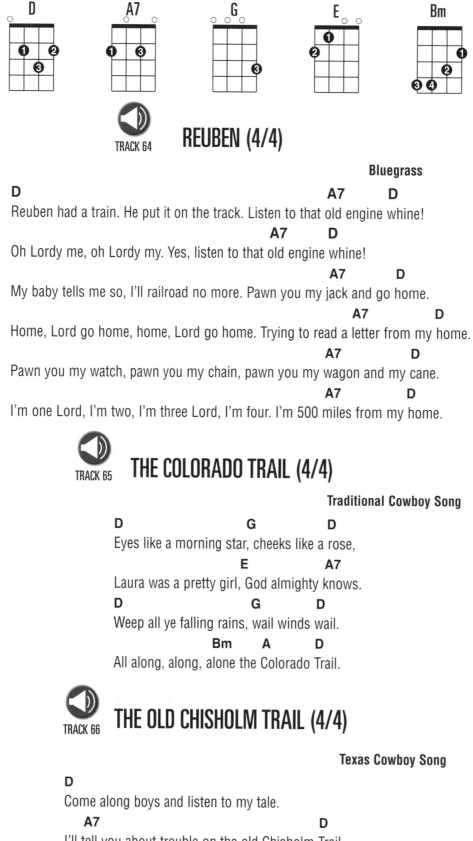

TRACK 64 **REUBEN (4/4)**

Bluegrass

D   **A7**   **D**
Reuben had a train. He put it on the track. Listen to that old engine whine!

                    A7   **D**
Oh Lordy me, oh Lordy my. Yes, listen to that old engine whine!

                    A7   **D**
My baby tells me so, I'll railroad no more. Pawn you my jack and go home.

                    A7   **D**
Home, Lord go home, home, Lord go home. Trying to read a letter from my home.

                    A7   **D**
Pawn you my watch, pawn you my chain, pawn you my wagon and my cane.

                    A7   **D**
I'm one Lord, I'm two, I'm three Lord, I'm four. I'm 500 miles from my home.

TRACK 65 **THE COLORADO TRAIL (4/4)**

Traditional Cowboy Song

D   **G**   **D**
Eyes like a morning star, cheeks like a rose,

           E   **A7**
Laura was a pretty girl, God almighty knows.

D   **G**   **D**
Weep all ye falling rains, wail winds wail.

           Bm   **A**   **D**
All along, along, alone the Colorado Trail.

TRACK 66 **THE OLD CHISHOLM TRAIL (4/4)**

Texas Cowboy Song

D
Come along boys and listen to my tale.

    A7   **D**
I'll tell you about trouble on the old Chisholm Trail.

        A7   **D**   **A7**   **D**
Come a ti-yi-yippee-yippee yay, yippee yay, come a ti-yi-yippee-yippie yay.

MINOR CHORDS CAN BE COOL

Let's take a look at some **minor chords** that will come in handy as you build your baritone chord vocabulary. You've already played several of them earlier in the book.

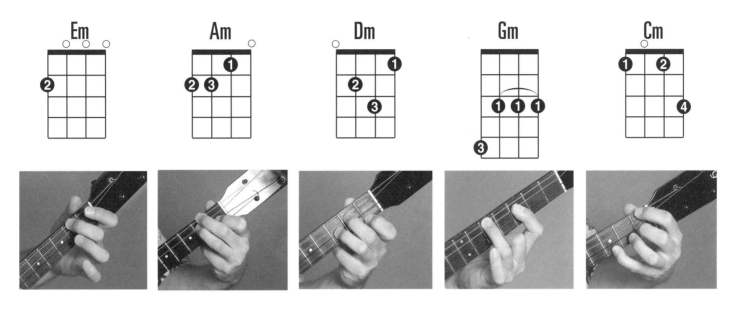

And here are some additional seventh chords we'll be pairing with our minor chords.

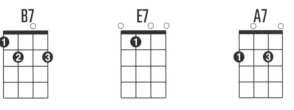

 TRACK 67

Let's start off in the key of E minor. Notice that it has the same key signature as G major: one sharp (F♯). E minor is the relative minor of G major.

TRACK 68

Now let's try a progression using A minor as its base. Strum four downstrokes per measure.

TRACK 69

Finally, we'll finish in G minor.

JUST FUN STRUMMING WITH MINOR CHORDS

Alright people! Let's make a joyful noise. This time, we're going to sit back and strum through one last little set of well-worn classics in the minor keys of E minor and D minor. These are the chords you'll be using. Notice there is one new chord, B♭.

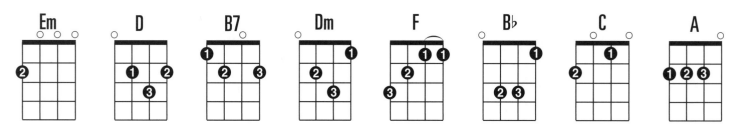

 SINNER MAN (4/4)

TRACK 70   **Traditional**

Em
Oh, sinner man, where you gonna run to?
D
Oh, sinner man, where you gonna run to?
Em   **D   Em**
Oh, sinner man, where you gonna run to on that day?

 **ZUM GALI GALI (4/4)**

TRACK 71   **Israeli Folk Song**

Em   B7   Em   **B7   Em**
Zum gali gali gali, zum gali gali. Zum gali gali gali, zum gali gali.
        B7   Em   **B7   Em**
Zum gali gali gali, zum gali gali. Zum gali gali gali, zum gali ga.
            B7   Em   **B7   Em**
He cha-lutz l'-ma-an a-vo-dah, a-vo-dah l'-ma-an he-cha-lutz.
            B7   Em   **B7   Em**
He cha-lutz l'-ma-an a-vo-dah, a-vo-dah l'-ma-an he-cha-lutz.

 THE DAYS OF '49 (4/4)

TRACK 72   **Spiritual**
Dm   **C**   **B♭   A   Dm**
I'm old Tom Moore from the bummer's shore in the good old golden days.
                              C   **B♭   A   Dm**
They call me a bummer and a ginsot too, but what care I for praise?
F   **A**
Wander 'round from town to town just like a roving sign.
    Dm   **C**   **B♭   A   Dm**
The people all say, "There goes Tom Moore, in the days of '49."
        F   **A**
In the days of old, in the days of gold, how oft times I repine.
    Dm   **C**   **B♭   A   Dm**
In the days of old when we dug up the gold in the days of '49.

If you enjoy the sound of playing in a minor key, here are some suggestions for songs that would make a great addition to any repertoire: "Summertime," "The House of the Rising Sun," "Wayfaring Stranger," "Blue Skies," "Scarborough Fair," "St. James Infirmary," and "Shady Grove," to name a few.

BARITONE UKULELE CHORD CHART

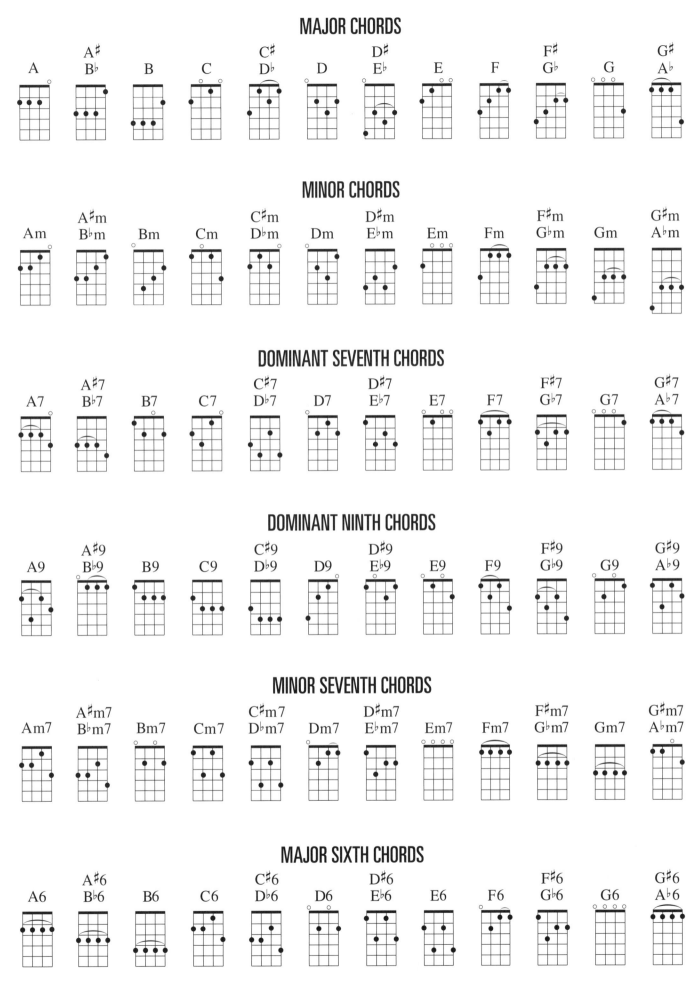

MINOR SIXTH CHORDS

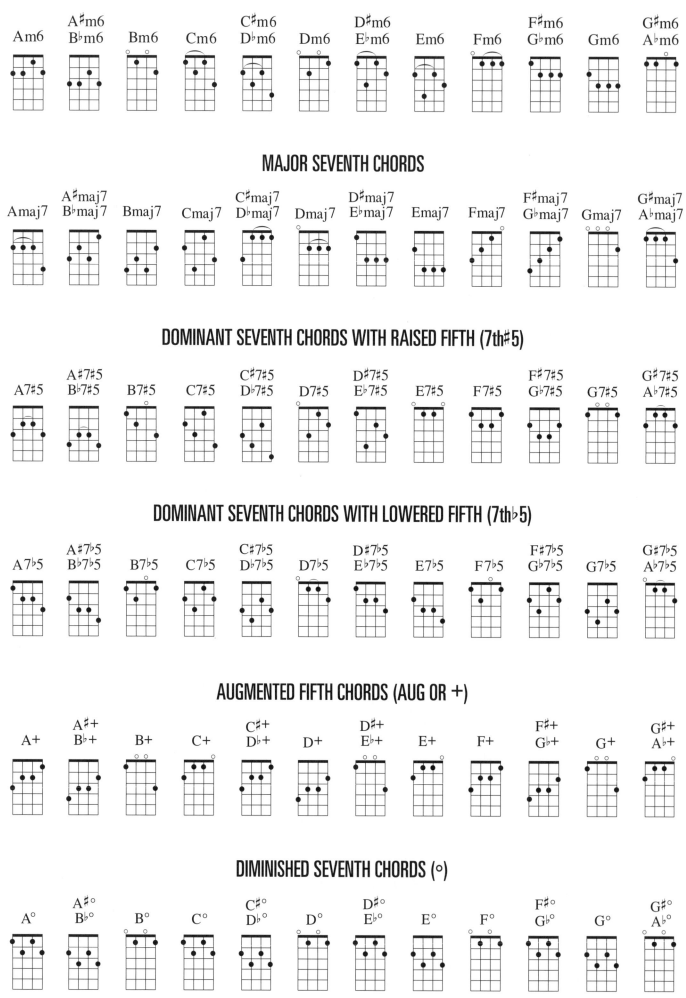

MAJOR SEVENTH CHORDS

DOMINANT SEVENTH CHORDS WITH RAISED FIFTH (7th#5)

DOMINANT SEVENTH CHORDS WITH LOWERED FIFTH (7th♭5)

AUGMENTED FIFTH CHORDS (AUG OR +)

DIMINISHED SEVENTH CHORDS (°)